Original title:
Joyful Mind

Copyright © 2024 Creative Arts Management OÜ
All rights reserved.

Author: Thor Castlebury
ISBN HARDBACK: 978-9916-88-206-1
ISBN PAPERBACK: 978-9916-88-207-8

A Garden of Gratitude

In the morning dew, petals gleam,
A whisper of thanks in each ray's beam.
Roots dig deep in the rich, dark earth,
Nature's embrace speaks of rebirth.

With every bloom, a story to tell,
In this sacred space, hearts swell.
Colors bright, a vibrant hue,
Grateful blooms, forever true.

Chasing the Light

Through shadows long, we find our way,
Seeking the dawn, the break of day.
Every step, a spark ignites,
Chasing dreams into the heights.

With every heartbeat, hope glows bright,
A journey marked by inner sight.
We rise, we soar, we fear no fall,
With courage clear, we heed the call.

The Playfulness of Dreams

In the quiet night, imaginations dance,
Whispers of wonders, a midnight chance.
Clouds like pillows, stars like toys,
Chasing the sounds of laughter and joys.

Through the fields of slumber we roam,
Sketching adventures, far from home.
With every dream, a new delight,
Playful spirits take their flight.

A Tapestry of Happiness

Threads of joy weave through the days,
In laughter shared, in sunlight's rays.
Colorful moments stitched with care,
Woven together, a life we share.

As time flows on, patterns emerge,
Celebrating love, a vibrant surge.
With every thread, a story spun,
In this tapestry, we are one.

Radiant Revelations

In the dawn's soft embrace, we rise,
Whispers of dreams dance in the skies.
Light spills over the waking ground,
With each heartbeat, hope is found.

Waves of colors begin to gleam,
Awakening the heart, igniting the dream.
Every shadow bears a silver lining,
In this moment, positivity shining.

Traces of Exuberance

Laughter echoes through the air,
Joy runs wild, without a care.
With every step, a rhythm plays,
In this vibrant dance, life sways.

Sparks of kindness, freely shared,
In each small act, love is declared.
Colors burst in a radiant show,
Embracing the warmth where hearts can grow.

The Bright Side of Clouds

Above, the clouds drift softly by,
Hiding secrets in the sky.
Yet behind each grey, there's a light,
A promise of warmth, shining bright.

When storms rage and shadows fall,
Hold on tight, for hope stands tall.
In their dance, a story unfolds,
With silver linings yet untold.

Petals of Positivity

Winds of change gently sway,
Spreading joy in a colorful array.
Each petal whispers words of grace,
Painting smiles on every face.

With every sunrise, new blooms appear,
Chasing away shadows, bringing cheer.
In every heart, a garden grows,
Nurtured by love, the sweetest prose.

A Tidal Wave of Warmth

The sun ignites the morning glow,
Waves of warmth in soft winds flow.
Hearts awaken to a bright embrace,
Nature dances, a soothing grace.

In each beam, a whisper sings,
Joyful laughter, the love it brings.
Like ocean tides that touch the shore,
A tidal wave that opens doors.

With every heartbeat, sunlight streams,
Kindled hopes and vibrant dreams.
Together, we can face the day,
In the warmth, we find our way.

So let the waves of love unite,
Bathe us in the golden light.
Through every challenge, we will rise,
A tidal wave beneath the skies.

The Garden of Grins

In a place where laughter blooms,
Joyful echoes chase the gloom.
Petals painted in vibrant hues,
A garden filled with friendly views.

Each smile is a flower bright,
Chasing shadows with pure delight.
Breezes carry giggles soft,
In this space, our spirits loft.

Sunsets sprinkle fairy dust,
Trust in love, it's life's must.
Together we'll sow seeds of cheer,
Harvesting smiles throughout the year.

With every bloom, our hearts will dance,
In this garden, take a chance.
Let the grins ignite the day,
In the warmth of joy, we stay.

Shawls of Happiness

Wrap me in your tender care,
Like a shawl, our love we share.
Soft and warm against the cold,
In your embrace, my heart is bold.

With every stitch, our memories weave,
A tapestry of joy to believe.
Colors bright and patterns fine,
In shawls of happiness, we shine.

Through chilly winds, we'll wander free,
Each layer warms both you and me.
In laughter's fabric and smiles spun,
Together we are two as one.

So drape me in this blissful thread,
With you, I'll never feel the dread.
In shawls of happiness, we'll reside,
Forever close, side by side.

Flickering Flames of Fun

Under the stars, we gather bright,
Flickering flames dance in the night.
Laughter echoes, shadows play,
Together we chase worries away.

Stories shared, memories made,
In the warmth, all fears do fade.
Sparks of joy light up our faces,
In this moment, happiness chases.

With every crackle, spirits soar,
Fun ignites, who could ask for more?
Dancing flames, our hearts align,
In flickering warmth, our souls entwine.

So let us toast to friendship true,
In flames of fun, I find you too.
Together beneath the starry dome,
In this magic, we feel at home.

Dances of Delight

In fields where wildflowers sway,
Dancing under the warm sun's ray.
Laughter echoes, spirits free,
In this joyous jubilee.

Whispers of the gentle wind,
Carrying dreams that never end.
Every step, a graceful flight,
Hearts entwined in sheer delight.

Colors burst in vibrant hue,
Painting skies of every blue.
Here we twirl, our souls ignite,
Lost in dances of delight.

Laughter in the Breeze

Softly flows the evening air,
Carrying laughter everywhere.
Children play, their voices rise,
Underneath the painted skies.

Tickling leaves and swaying trees,
Whisper secrets with the breeze.
Sunset's glow, a warm embrace,
Time stands still in this sweet space.

Moments shared, a joyful sound,
In this paradise we've found.
Nature sings, our hearts agree,
With laughter dancing in the breeze.

Serenade of Light

Moonlight weaves a silver thread,
Guiding dreams where lovers tread.
Stars emerge and softly glow,
Whispering secrets, hearts aglow.

Candles flicker, shadows play,
In this serenade, we sway.
Every note, a gentle sigh,
As the night begins to fly.

Melodies of peace unfold,
In this magic, we are bold.
Together in this lovely night,
Lost in tunes of pure delight.

Glimmers of Happiness

In the morning's golden light,
Every moment shines so bright.
With each smile that we share,
Happiness dances in the air.

Footsteps on a winding path,
Chasing joy, escaping wrath.
With laughter ringing, hearts in tune,
Glimmers sparkle like the moon.

Friendship blooms in every place,
Bringing warmth, a sweet embrace.
In life's journey, hand in hand,
We find happiness, like grains of sand.

Chasing Sunbeams

In the early morning light,
We run with hearts so free,
Dancing on the golden edge,
Chasing down each sunbeam.

Through the fields where daisies bloom,
We laugh and spin around,
Every shadow fades away,
Joy in every sound.

In the warmth of summer's glow,
We find our spirits soar,
Hand in hand, we chase the glow,
And dream of evermore.

A Garden of Glee

In a garden filled with light,
Colors vivid, oh so bright,
Flowers dance in gentle sway,
Whispers of a joyful day.

Buzzing bees and songbirds sing,
Nature's beauty, life's pure spring,
Every petal holds a dream,
In this wondrous, vibrant scheme.

Children laugh and play around,
In this paradise we've found,
Each moment filled with glee,
In our hearts, forever free.

Melodies of Merriment

Play the flute, the drum, the harp,
Listen close, hear every spark,
Notes that twirl like autumn leaves,
Crafting joy that never leaves.

Laughter dances in the air,
Songs of love and sweet despair,
With each chord, our spirits rise,
Melodies that mesmerize.

Filling hearts with pure delight,
Echoing through day and night,
Harmony forever sings,
In the tales that music brings.

The Art of Contentment

In a quiet, still embrace,
Find the peace, a sacred space,
Moments rich, like autumn gold,
Simple joys, a sight to behold.

Sipping tea in evening light,
Watching stars emerge from night,
Breath by breath, we find our way,
Grateful hearts in calm display.

Contentment blooms in gentle ways,
Teaches us to cherish days,
In the silence, wisdom speaks,
In each heartbeat, love's unique.

The Sunshine Trail

Beneath bright skies we wander wide,
With golden rays that softly guide.
Through fields of green and blossoms bright,
We follow dreams in pure delight.

The trail ahead, a shimmering path,
Inviting smiles and joyful laughs.
Each step we take, a story unfolds,
In the warmth of sun, our hearts uphold.

With every turn, new wonders greet,
The world around feels bright and sweet.
Nature's song, a gentle call,
As we embrace the joy of it all.

So hand in hand, we stroll along,
In harmony with nature's song.
Forever on this sunny quest,
Together, we shall be our best.

Skipping Shadows

In twilight's hush, we start to play,
As shadows dance, they lead the way.
With laughter light, we flit and fly,
   Creating magic 'neath the sky.

The moonlight twirls in gleaming beams,
While whispers weave through our sweet dreams.
Each step a skip, a chance to soar,
Among the whispers, spirits roar.

We chase the dark, embrace the night,
As shadows flicker in soft light.
Together bound, we leap and twist,
In this joyous, fleeting mist.

So come, dear friend, let's chase the dawn,
Dance with shadows till they're gone.
In every step, a new delight,
We weave the magic of the night.

A Tapestry of Triumphs

With courage stitched into each seam,
We thread our hopes, we weave our dream.
In vibrant hues our stories blend,
A tapestry our hearts defend.

Each triumph born from trials faced,
In moments lost, in dreams embraced.
With woven threads of joy and pain,
Our lives are rich with love's sweet gain.

The fabric glows with lessons learned,
Through every twist, our spirits turned.
In unity, we find our strength,
A tapestry that knows no length.

So let us share this art we create,
As life's grand patterns resonate.
Together we will craft and strive,
In this rich weave, we all thrive.

Enchanted Moments

In quiet woods, we wander free,
Where whispers dance among the trees.
The sun dips low, a golden hue,
Each moment steals our hearts anew.

A brook hums soft, with tales untold,
As petals drift, like dreams of old.
Beneath a sky of azure blue,
Enchanted moments shared by two.

The fireflies light the dusky air,
Each flicker holds a whispered prayer.
With gentle hearts, our spirits soar,
In these sweet hours, we crave no more.

As shadows blend with twilight's grace,
We find in silence, our safe space.
With every breath, love's essence flows,
In enchanted moments, our spirit grows.

The Sweetness of Being

In morning light, the dewdrops gleam,
Awakening the day like a dream.
A gentle breeze, a soft embrace,
Reminds us of our sacred place.

With laughter bright, our hearts align,
In simple joys, like sips of wine.
Each fleeting glance, a treasure rare,
The sweetness found, in moments shared.

As petals fall from blooming trees,
We gather love, like summer's breeze.
With open arms, the world we see,
In every breath, the sweetness of being.

As twilight paints the skies with grace,
We dance in dreams, a soft embrace.
With gratitude, we cherish these,
These moments spent beneath the trees.

Sails of Serenity

On calm blue seas, our hearts set sail,
With whispered winds, we catch the gale.
The horizon calls, a soft retreat,
In sails of serenity, our souls meet.

With every wave, a story grows,
As salty air, our spirit knows.
Together bound, we face the sun,
In this vast world, we are but one.

The sun dips low, a fiery glow,
With stars aglow, our dreams will flow.
In tranquil nights, we find our peace,
In sails of serenity, love won't cease.

As moonlight dances on the tide,
We hold the warmth of love inside.
With open hearts, we drift away,
In sails of serenity, forever stay.

Waves of Wonderment

On shores of gold, the waves roll high,
In playful dance, they touch the sky.
Each splash a song, a joyful cheer,
In waves of wonderment, we feel near.

The tide brings whispers from afar,
Of hidden dreams and every star.
With footprints imprinted in the sand,
Together we embark, hand in hand.

As seagulls sing in skies of gray,
We chase the light in every play.
With open hearts, the world we free,
In waves of wonderment, just you and me.

With moonlit nights and starlit skies,
We trace the path where magic lies.
In every wave that breaks the shore,
In waves of wonderment, we explore.

Moments Wrapped in Bliss

Soft whispers in the night,
Glimmers of the moonlight bright,
Hearts entwined, a gentle sigh,
In this moment, we can fly.

Time stands still, a fleeting blink,
In your eyes, the stars do wink,
Lost in dreams, we drift away,
Here together, come what may.

Every heartbeat tells a tale,
Love's sweet wind fills up the sail,
Wrapped in warmth, forever near,
In this bliss, there's naught to fear.

As the world begins to fade,
In our hearts, a secret made,
Holding close, we cherish each,
Moments wrapped, our souls in reach.

The Laughter of Clouds

Fluffy white on a canvas blue,
Dancing lightly, drifting through,
Whispers soft, a gentle sound,
In their laugh, joy can be found.

Raindrops fall, a playful tease,
Kissing earth with such sweet ease,
In the sky, their giggles ring,
Nature's song, the heart will sing.

Sunset hues, a brilliant show,
Clouds aglow, as day will go,
Cascades of light, a fleeting chase,
In their laughter, we find grace.

Every shape tells a story bold,
In their arms, warmth to behold,
They float on by, just like a dream,
In their joy, we too can beam.

A Kaleidoscope of Smiles

Colors swirl in vibrant play,
Each smile brings a brighter day,
In the mirror, joy reflects,
A dance of life, with no regrets.

Children laugh in pure delight,
Sharing joy, their hearts ignite,
Bright and warm like summer sun,
Kaleidoscope, we're all as one.

Friends gather, stories shared,
In each moment, love declared,
Life's mosaic, piece by piece,
A canvas where our troubles cease.

In the chaos, find the grace,
In each smile, a warm embrace,
Together now, we light the way,
In a world where we can play.

Serenity in a Cup

Steam rises with a gentle grace,
In this warmth, I find my space,
Savoring each calming sip,
Life slows down, time's sweet trip.

A cozy chair, the world outside,
In this moment, worries hide,
Jasmine blooms and honey's kiss,
In this cup, I taste pure bliss.

Minds unburdened, spirits soar,
In their depths, I seek for more,
Flavors dance, a symphony,
In this brew, I feel so free.

As the sun begins to set,
In my heart, no room for fret,
With each sip, a soft release,
Finding calm, a sweetest peace.

Constellations of Content

In the darkest sky we find,
Stars like thoughts that truly shine,
Mapping dreams with gentle care,
Constellations bloom up there.

Every twinkle, every light,
Holds a secret, pure and bright,
Whispers soft of joy and peace,
In their glow, all sorrows cease.

Waves of wonder, currents flow,
Guiding hearts where feelings grow,
In this night, no fears unfold,
Magic tales of warmth retold.

Bright horizons, endless grace,
Fill the night with warm embrace,
In the calm, our spirits soar,
Finding solace evermore.

Starlight Smiles

Glimmers dance on velvet skies,
Starlight whispers, hush replies,
Every beam a joyful spark,
Painting dreams within the dark.

Laughter echoes, soft and clear,
Moonlit paths that draw us near,
In the night, we share a glance,
Caught in cosmic, sweet romance.

Each moment glows, a treasure bright,
Guiding souls with pure delight,
Every twinkle, every beam,
Fills our hearts and fuels our dream.

Through the cosmos, love will guide,
Hand in hand, we'll walk this ride,
Chasing starlight, hearts aligned,
In this magic, love defined.

The Heart's Craft

With every beat, a brushstroke made,
Painting love that won't soon fade,
A canvas spun with threads of gold,
In the heart, true art unfolds.

Chasing dreams, we carve each day,
Through the shadows, light will play,
Each emotion, a stroke divine,
Crafted in this heart of mine.

Vivid colors, soft and bold,
Stories whispered, truths retold,
In this workshop of our souls,
Love, the art that makes us whole.

As we build this world so bright,
Every moment feels so right,
In each heartbeat, life's sweet craft,
Love's embrace, a gentle draft.

A Festival of Feelings

Gather round, the night is young,
Songs of joy, we've just begun,
Feelings swirl in melodies,
In this dance, our hearts find ease.

Laughter fills the starry air,
Every glance, a tender care,
Colors burst in sheer delight,
Celebration through the night.

Whispers soft of dreams awake,
In this fest, our hearts will break
Into fragments, love proclaimed,
In the night, we'll not be tamed.

Join the chorus, sing your part,
Let the music lift your heart,
In this gathering of souls,
Feelings reign as joy unfolds.

The Rhythm of Radiance

In the dawn's gentle glow,
Light dances through the trees,
Whispers of wind, soft and low,
Nature's song puts hearts at ease.

Colors splash across the sky,
As day breaks into cheer,
Joyful notes, as birds fly high,
Each moment feels so clear.

Shadows fade with the sun's rise,
Hope blooms in vibrant hues,
The world shakes off its disguise,
Awakening to new views.

In this flow, we find our way,
Guided by a radiant beam,
Every moment a bright play,
Life unfolds like a dream.

Moments of Magic

Beneath the shimmering stars,
Whispers of silence reign,
Time pauses, healing scars,
Each heartbeat is a gain.

Glimmers of laughter and light,
Dance across the night sky,
In dreams, the world feels right,
Our spirits lift and fly.

A glance turns into a spell,
Connections spark like fire,
In our hearts, stories swell,
Chasing what we desire.

These moments, fleeting yet bright,
We cherish them like song,
In darkness, we find the light,
Together we belong.

Embracing the Intangible

In the hush of day's first breath,
Feelings linger in the air,
A bond that knows no death,
Connections hidden with care.

A smile shared, a glance exchanged,
Footprints left on hearts anew,
In the quiet, lives are changed,
Magic flows in all we do.

Not all treasures can be seen,
Wisdom wrapped in gentle sway,
In the in-between and unseen,
Love guides us on our way.

With open arms, we find our path,
Navigating the unknown,
In this dance, we share our laugh,
Creating a world we've grown.

A Chorus of Cheerfulness

The morning sun starts to rise,
With cheer that fills the sky,
Laughter echoes, joyful cries,
As birds begin to fly.

Gathered here in this embrace,
Hearts beat in perfect time,
In each smile, a warm grace,
Life's rhythm is a rhyme.

Together we weave our song,
Melodies lift us high,
With every note, we belong,
United, we can fly.

In moments shared, we find our way,
A chorus strong and true,
With love like sunlight each day,
Together, me and you.

Sunlit Pathways

Golden rays kiss the earth,
Winding paths in the green,
Nature whispers its mirth,
Life's beauty, brightly seen.

Butterflies flutter near,
Dancing on petals bright,
Every moment so dear,
Bathed in warm, golden light.

Shadows play on the ground,
As trees sway with the breeze,
In this haven we've found,
Time slows with such sweet ease.

Footsteps echo with glee,
As we wander along,
With hearts wild and so free,
We embrace nature's song.

The Dance of Serenity

Moonlight spills soft and clear,
Upon the tranquil scene,
Whispers of the night near,
The world feels so serene.

Stars twinkle like old friends,
In the velvet sky's embrace,
Time as gently it bends,
In this peaceful space.

With each breath we can feel,
The calmness in the air,
A moment that's so real,
Our worries stripped bare.

In stillness, we unite,
Two souls gently collide,
In the calm of the night,
With nothing to hide.

Threads of Thrill

Tangled vines of bright hue,
Climbing up ancient walls,
Each corner hides something new,
Adventure softly calls.

The rush of the cool breeze,
Retreats into the wild,
Nature's grand mysteries,
Always make me feel like a child.

On a quest, we will find,
The magic in the air,
As we leave doubts behind,
Seeking treasures with care.

In laughter, we will soar,
With hearts full of delight,
Together, we'll explore,
In the glow of the night.

Wonders of Whimsy

In a land where dreams play,
Colors swirl in the sky,
Imagination's ballet,
Where laughter learns to fly.

Bubbles float with a glee,
Dancing in sunlit streams,
Every moment feels free,
A tapestry of dreams.

The odd and the bizarre,
Paints a world full of cheer,
Magic within a jar,
Whispers of joy so near.

Unicorns prance with grace,
In fields of endless cheer,
Let's journey to that place,
Where whimsy draws us near.

Brimming with Bliss

In the garden where flowers bloom,
Joy dances in every room.
The laughter of children fills the air,
Every moment a treasure, bright and rare.

Chasing shadows of clouds above,
Hearts entwined with warmth and love.
A gentle breeze whispers sweet delight,
As day turns softly into night.

Colors swirl like a painter's dream,
Life flows like a winding stream.
With each heartbeat, cherish this place,
In the arms of joy, we find our grace.

Everlasting Echoes

Whispers linger in the still,
Memories dance and hearts fulfill.
In the silence, stories bloom,
Echoes of laughter fill the room.

Time weaves its intricate thread,
Carrying whispers of things unsaid.
With every tick of the clock we find,
The ties that bind, love intertwined.

Stars twinkle, stories unfold,
Lasting echoes, treasures untold.
In the quiet, we softly sigh,
Holding close the moments that fly.

The Warmth of Whimsy

A playful breeze, a gentle tease,
Leaves sway lightly in their ease.
Bright colors beckon, come and play,
In a world where dreams sway.

Laughter bubbles like a stream,
The heart awakens with a gleam.
Every corner hides a surprise,
Magic glimmers in our eyes.

With a flick of the wrist, joy flows,
Unraveled in the light that glows.
Whimsy dances, sweet and free,
Embracing life's simple glee.

The Serenade of Sunshine

Sunbeams spill like liquid gold,
Caressing flowers, bright and bold.
Nature sings a sweet refrain,
As joy awakens after rain.

Golden rays kiss the earth,
Celebrating each moment of birth.
A symphony of light and cheer,
The sun's warm hug draws us near.

Under skies of azure hue,
Life dances in each vibrant view.
With every heartbeat, we align,
In the serenade of sunshine.

Sparkles of Serenity

In the hush of dawn's embrace,
Whispers float on gentle air.
Calmness dances, soft and clear,
Nature's grace, beyond compare.

Rippling streams of silver light,
Petals brush against the breeze.
In this haven, hearts take flight,
Finding solace, sweet release.

Mountains rise in tranquil hues,
Rays of sun begin to glow.
Every shadow fades from view,
In this peace, our spirits grow.

Stars appear in velvet night,
Guiding dreams with twinkling spark.
In the stillness, all feels right,
Serenity's soft remark.

Effervescent Dreams

Bubbles rise in twilight skies,
Laughter dances on the waves.
Every wish begins to fly,
In this world where joy enslaves.

Neon colors, vibrant schemes,
Paint the canvas of our minds.
Waking softly from our dreams,
Reality's sweet intertwines.

Echoes bounce in heart's delight,
Sparkling moments, never fade.
In this magic, hearts ignite,
Memories that we have made.

Chasing flickers of the night,
With each heartbeat, hope resumes.
Together, we embrace the light,
In this well of effervescent blooms.

Echoes of Euphoria

Through the fields where laughter rings,
Joyful shouts weave through the air.
Every heartbeat softly sings,
Life embraces, free from care.

Moments cherished, sweet reprise,
As the sun begins to set.
In this bliss, our spirits rise,
Finding joy, we won't forget.

Whispers dance in twilight's glow,
Every star, a tale to tell.
In this magic, time moves slow,
Echoes weave a soothing swell.

With each breath, the world unfolds,
A tapestry of love and cheer.
In these echoes, pure and bold,
Euphoria's embrace is here.

The Glow of Gratitude

In the morning's tender light,
A soft glow begins to rise.
Thankful hearts take joyful flight,
Beneath vast and open skies.

Moments shared in gentle grace,
Every smile, a warmth bestowed.
In this life, we find our place,
Gratitude's path gently showed.

Whispers of the night remind,
Every star, a gift divine.
In the stillness, souls aligned,
Grateful hearts in love entwine.

With each breath, we honor time,
Embracing all that life imparts.
In this glow, we find the rhyme,
Gratitude, the song of hearts.

A Symphony of Smiles

In the morning light, they gleam,
A sparkle bright, like a dream.
Laughter dances, spirits high,
Whispers of joy, soaring nigh.

Faces glow with tales untold,
Each smile a treasure, pure and gold.
Warmth spreads wide, hearts interlace,
In this symphony, love finds its place.

Notes of kindness gently play,
Chasing the shadows of the day.
Together we weave harmony,
A chorus sweet, wild, and free.

So let us share this bright refrain,
Through smiles, we conquer every pain.
A melody of souls, aligned,
In laughter's echo, joy we find.

Vibrations of Bliss

A gentle breeze through the trees,
Carries whispers of sweet ease.
Each moment a soft embrace,
Time slows down, a sacred space.

In the echoes of laughter, we sway,
Finding light in the everyday.
With every heartbeat, pure delight,
A dance of souls, so vibrant, bright.

Colors blend in the evening glow,
As skies ignite with a fiery show.
Together we sing, hearts aglow,
In vibrations of bliss, we overflow.

Let worries fade like distant sound,
In this tranquil haven, peace is found.
With every breath, we rise and soar,
In blissful harmony, forevermore.

The Canvas of Cheer

Brushstrokes of laughter paint the day,
Colors of joy in bright display.
Every moment, a hue of glee,
Creating a masterpiece, wild and free.

Sunshine drips from the sky so blue,
Filling the world with every hue.
In every heart, a smile to share,
Writing stories beyond compare.

Swirls of happiness fill the air,
Captured in moments, beyond compare.
Life's canvas wide, we dance and play,
Creating memories, come what may.

With colors bold, we find our way,
Painting a joy that will forever stay.
In the gallery of life, we cheer,
Each brushstroke a treasure we hold dear.

Delightful Reflections

In the stillness of the night,
Stars shimmer with soft light.
Taking time to pause and see,
Reflections of who we can be.

Every glance holds a precious truth,
Moments cherished, frozen youth.
In the mirror, hearts intertwine,
Delightful glimpses, pure and divine.

Whispers of hope on gentle waves,
Guiding the lost, the hearts it saves.
With every breath, we find our sound,
In the laughter, joy is found.

So let us dance in these reflections,
Embracing love and connections.
For in every beat, a chance to rise,
Delightful echoes that never dies.

Radiant Reflections

In mirrors bright, the shadows dance,
A glimpse of light, a fleeting chance.
Each ripple tells of dreams untold,
In silence deep, their secrets hold.

The sunbeams break on waters clear,
In every wave, a world sincere.
Through gleaming glass, I seek my soul,
In radiant hues, I feel whole.

The colors swirl, a vibrant play,
Like whispers soft at end of day.
In twilight's grace, reflections gleam,
A canvas brushed with every dream.

So let me dive in depths unseen,
Where echoes fade, and hearts convene.
With every glance, a story grows,
In radiant paths, my spirit flows.

A Glimpse of Elysium

In gardens vast, where roses bloom,
The air is sweet, dispelling gloom.
Each petal soft, a breath of peace,
In nature's heart, my worries cease.

The golden light through branches streams,
A tapestry of vivid dreams.
With scent of earth and sky so blue,
In Elysium, I find what's true.

The gentle breeze sings soft refrain,
A melody that soothes the brain.
I wander through this tranquil space,
Embraced by joy, a warm embrace.

In moments shared with skies so wide,
I find the love that cannot hide.
With every breath in paradise,
A glimpse of bliss, a sweet surprise.

Radiance of Thought

In stillness waits a spark divine,
A whispered truth, a thread of time.
Within my mind, the colors flow,
In radiant thought, the visions grow.

Each idea born in shadows bright,
Illuminates the darkest night.
A dance of muse, a painter's hand,
Creating worlds, both vast and grand.

Embrace the light, let worries fade,
In every glance, a plan is laid.
The brilliance shines in paths unknown,
Within my heart, the seeds are sown.

Through visions clear, the future gleams,
In every turn, the spirit beams.
With radiance of thought, we rise,
To touch the stars, beyond the skies.

Whispers of Elation

In morning's glow, a soft embrace,
The whispers tease, a gentle grace.
With laughter light as autumn leaves,
In every note, the heart believes.

The world alive, in colors brave,
With every joy, our spirits wave.
Through playful winds, our dreams take flight,
In harmony, we chase the light.

With every step, the echoes sing,
Of moments bright that joy can bring.
In whispers sweet, our hopes align,
In elation's dance, the stars will shine.

So let us rise with hearts aglow,
Embracing all that life can show.
In every breath, a joyous song,
With whispers loud, we all belong.

Vanilla Skies and Euphoria

Under a blanket of soft cream light,
Whispers of dreams float through the night.
A gentle breeze carries sweet delight,
As hearts awaken to a new sight.

Clouds like pillows drift in the air,
Cradling wishes without a care.
Moments of bliss spark everywhere,
In the embrace of love's warm stare.

Golden rays dance on the horizon,
Filling the world with hope's beacon.
With every glance, the spirit's risen,
In vanilla skies, our hearts deepen.

As day unfolds with colors bright,
We chase the echoes of pure light.
Together we soar, spirited flight,
In euphoria, we lose all fright.

Blossoms of the Heart

Petals unfurl, soft and bright,
In gardens where dreams take flight.
Each bloom whispers sweet embrace,
A story written in nature's grace.

Veins of color pulse with life,
Overcoming the shadows of strife.
In the dance of sun and rain,
Love flourishes, breaks the chain.

A fragrance lingers in the air,
Soft reminders of moments rare.
Every blossom speaks a song,
In the heart's garden, we belong.

As seasons change, we find our way,
Through winding paths of light and gray.
With each new bud, our hopes restart,
In the endless blossoms of the heart.

Curious Skies of Joy

Above the world, a canvas sprawls,
In hues of wonder, nature calls.
Clouds parade in shapes so fleet,
Carrying laughter on the wind's heartbeat.

Stars sprinkle sparkle, twinkling bright,
Guiding travelers through the night.
Each glance upward sparks delight,
In curious skies, our spirits ignite.

The sun peaks in a playful game,
Chasing shadows, setting flame.
With every dawn, new tales arise,
In the embrace of vast blue skies.

With every cloud that drifts on by,
We find new dreams, we learn to fly.
In joyful bounds, we claim our space,
Under the curious skies, we find our place.

A Journey through Laughter

Steps echoing in the morning light,
With every chuckle, spirits take flight.
We traverse paths of joy and play,
In laughter's embrace, we find our way.

With friends beside, we dance and sing,
Moments woven into everything.
Every smile shared, a treasure bestowed,
On this vibrant, whimsical road.

Through valleys low and mountains high,
We chase the dreams that never die.
In echoes of joy, our hearts will sway,
Together, in laughter, we find our way.

As stars emerge and day drifts out,
Our giggles linger, filling the clout.
In this journey, hand in hand tight,
We weave our tales under starlit night.

Blossoms of Happiness

In gardens bright, the flowers bloom,
Their colors bright, dispel the gloom.
Joy dances lightly on gentle breeze,
Whispering secrets through the trees.

With every petal, dreams arise,
Reflecting light from sunny skies.
Their fragrance sweet, a soft embrace,
Filling hearts with warmth and grace.

Beneath the sun, laughter rings,
Nature sings of joyful things.
In this moment, worries cease,
Blossoms spread their sweet, sweet peace.

Dancing shadows in golden light,
Chasing away the edges of night.
Here in the garden, hope is found,
In blossoms bright, joy knows no bound.

The Dance of Merriment

The stars above begin to glow,
As laughter weaves, and breezes blow.
In a circle, friends take their stand,
Together they twirl, hand in hand.

The music plays, a joyous sound,
Feet leap lightly from the ground.
In every spin, the spirits soar,
Merriment knocks at every door.

With every step, the world grows bright,
In this moment, hearts take flight.
Their smiles like sunbeams fill the air,
Bubbles of joy, without a care.

As the night fades into day,
Memories spark in bright array.
The dance of life, forever free,
A tapestry of harmony.

Echoes of Elation

In highlands green, the voices rise,
Echoes of laughter touch the skies.
Each note a treasure, soft and clear,
A song of joy, for all to hear.

Through valleys deep, the sounds resound,
Carried forth, their beauty found.
With every echo, hearts ignite,
Sparkling dreams in the moonlight.

In the distance, the laughter swells,
Chiming notes like ringing bells.
Every moment, a jubilant glow,
A symphony of what we know.

Together, we weave a tale so bright,
In the echoes, pure delight.
Holding tightly to what we share,
In these echoes, love fills the air.

Canvas of Cheer

A canvas stretched, in colors bold,
Brush strokes shimmer, tales unfold.
Each hue a smile, a fleeting glance,
Painted joy in a lively dance.

The sun's warm rays, a golden hue,
Splash of laughter in skies so blue.
With every stroke, a heart's delight,
Creating wonders in warm sunlight.

In the gallery, moments gleam,
Captured whispers, lost in dream.
Through the art, we find our way,
In vibrant colors, night and day.

Together we celebrate this life,
A masterpiece, free from strife.
On this canvas, our spirits soar,
In strokes of cheer, forevermore.

The Lightness of Being

In morning's glow, we find our way,
With whispered hopes that gently sway.
The air is soft, the world anew,
In every breath, a dream of blue.

We dance with shadows, light as air,
With laughter ringing everywhere.
The heart unfolds in sweet release,
Embracing life, a fleeting peace.

Moments flutter like a feather,
In sunlit skies, we're light as a tether.
No weight to bear, just joy and cheer,
In this delight, we lose all fear.

Together, we let worries flee,
In the lightness, we find our free.
With open hearts and spirits bright,
We soar above, into the light.

Colors of Affection

A canvas painted bright and bold,
With strokes of love, our stories told.
Each hue a whisper, soft and clear,
In every shade, I hold you near.

Crimson blush of passion's kiss,
Emerald green, the heart's sweet bliss.
In golden rays, our laughter shines,
In purple twilight, our souls entwine.

With every color, a bond we weave,
In vibrant moments, we believe.
A rainbow formed by dreams we chase,
In every heart, a sacred space.

As shadows fade and daylight streams,
We find ourselves in each other's dreams.
With colors bright and spirits high,
Together, we paint the endless sky.

An Afternoon of Carefree Thoughts

Beneath the trees, where silence sings,
We drift on clouds, on feathered wings.
Each moment breathes a gentle sigh,
In sunny warmth, the hours fly.

With laughter scattered like warm light,
Our worries fade, the future bright.
We float on whispers, soft as air,
In blissful moments, free from care.

Time slows down in this sacred space,
With every glance, a sweet embrace.
Thoughts meander like a stream,
In this afternoon, we live the dream.

Together here, nothing to fear,
With carefree hearts, we draw it near.
An hour spent in love's sweet thrall,
In each other's joy, we have it all.

The Whisper of Possibility

In quiet moments, dreams unfold,
A whispered promise, soft and bold.
With every breath, a chance to rise,
To touch the stars, to claim the skies.

The world is vast, with paths unknown,
In shadows deep, the seeds are sown.
Each choice we make, a step we dare,
To chase a vision, light as air.

With open hearts, we seek the new,
In every heartbeat, hope shines through.
Possibilities gently dance and sway,
Inviting us to find our way.

In the stillness, we hear the call,
Of dreams awaiting, beyond the wall.
With courage found, we'll take the leap,
In the whisper of life, our souls will reap.

Whispers of Delight

In the quiet of the morn,
Soft whispers fill the air,
Dancing leaves on gentle breeze,
Nature's song, a loving care.

Petals open to the sun,
Every color sings its tune,
In the garden, joy begun,
A sweet symphony in bloom.

Hearts awaken with each note,
As laughter echoes far and wide,
Embracing life, a gentle boat,
On waves of love, we glide.

Moments cherished, never missed,
In the whispers, we find light,
A tender touch, a fleeting kiss,
Delight shines ever so bright.

A Symphony of Laughter

In a room where laughter flows,
Melodies of joy arise,
Every giggle, every pose,
Creates a song beneath the skies.

Echoes dance from wall to wall,
A chorus of hearts intertwined,
In this moment, we stand tall,
With harmony, our spirits aligned.

Through the trials, through the tears,
Laughter weaves a golden thread,
Binding souls and calming fears,
With each chuckle, joy is spread.

Together, we sing as one,
A symphony that won't depart,
In every note, love's work is done,
In laughter, we find our heart.

Radiance in the Everyday

Morning light spills on the floor,
Golden beams dance on the wall,
In mundane shapes, we explore,
Finding beauty in it all.

A cup of tea, a quiet sigh,
Moments simple, yet profound,
With every glance towards the sky,
Joy is wrapped in what we've found.

Children playing, laughter free,
Colors splash in vibrant play,
In the noise, tranquility,
Radiance in the everyday.

In the fleeting, in the small,
Beauty shines in humble ways,
Life unfolds, a precious call,
In the light, our spirit stays.

The Sparkle of Sunlight

Morning breaks with golden rays,
The world awakes, a vibrant scene,
Nature's brush paints bright arrays,
  The sparkle of sunlight, serene.

Gentle flickers on the stream,
A diamond dance upon the blue,
In the warmth, our hearts redeem,
  Finding hope in every hue.

Fields of gold, the wind does sigh,
A soft embrace, a sweet delight,
With every beam, our spirits fly,
Chasing shadows, seeking light.

In the twilight, hues of blush,
The sun descends with tender grace,
A final sparkle in the hush,
We find our peace in nature's face.

A Palette of Pleasures

Colors dance in the sky,
Whispers of joy float by.
Each hue sings a sweet song,
In this world, we belong.

Sunset paints with gentle grace,
A warm light on every face.
Laughter spills like vibrant paint,
A moment pure, without constraint.

The heart's canvas wide and free,
Happiness flows like the sea.
With every stroke, life ignites,
Creating magic in the nights.

Together in this beauty found,
Where love and cheer abound.
A palette rich, a joyful sight,
In every blend, pure delight.

Glorious Connections

Hands reach out, seeking warmth,
In this dance, a tender charm.
Eyes meet like stars aligned,
A bond so rare, so refined.

Words spoken, soft as air,
Promises shared, beyond compare.
Hearts entwined like vines that climb,
In sync, we flow, through space and time.

A melody of souls combined,
In laughter's echo, love defined.
Each moment blooms, a sacred trust,
In glorious connections, we must.

Through stormy skies or sunny days,
Together, we'll find our ways.
In unity, forever strong,
In this together, we belong.

Bubbles of Bliss

Bubbles float in the air,
Each a dream, beyond compare.
Glimmers catch the golden light,
Fleeting joys, oh what a sight!

Children laugh, they chase and play,
Innocence brightens up the day.
With each pop, a memory made,
In this moment, fears allayed.

Joy in simple, swirling forms,
A dance of color, nature's charms.
In their rise, find peace and cheer,
Bubbles burst, our smiles appear.

As they vanish, softly sigh,
In our hearts, the laughter lies.
The magic lives, forever kissed,
In the bubbles of our bliss.

A Celebration of Simplicity

In quiet moments, life unfolds,
The beauty in the small it holds.
A gentle breeze, a blooming flower,
In simplicity, we find our power.

A cup of tea, warm hands embrace,
In this stillness, we find our place.
Conversations soft as whispers,
In the mundane, joy occurs.

Stars above in a velvet night,
Guiding hearts with their soft light.
In every breath, a treasure found,
In simple joys, our hearts are bound.

Let us pause and take it in,
The magic where all lives begin.
In a world of chaos, be the light,
A celebration of what feels right.

Glows of Gratitude

In the morning light, we rise,
With thankful hearts, we reach for skies.
Each moment shared, a precious gift,
In gratitude, our spirits lift.

Nature whispers, soft and clear,
Love surrounds us, ever near.
The warmth of friends, the joy of peace,
In thankful hearts, our worries cease.

A simple touch, a kind hello,
In little things, our blessings grow.
We find the good in every day,
With each breath, we choose to stay.

Underneath the starry dome,
In gratitude, we find our home.
A promise made, to hold this light,
In glows of gratitude, we shine so bright.

The Harmony of Elation

Beneath the sky, we dance along,
With laughter's notes, our hearts are strong.
Each step we take, a joyful sound,
In harmony, we are unbound.

The breeze it sings a sweet refrain,
A melody that eases pain.
In every smile, a spark of grace,
In elation, we find our place.

The world alive, a vibrant hue,
In colors bright, we start anew.
With open arms, we greet the day,
In harmony, we laugh and play.

Through highs and lows, our spirits soar,
Together always, forevermore.
In elation's arms, we turn and twirl,
With hearts embraced, we paint the world.

Free Spirits of Ecstasy

In twilight's glow, we take our flight,
With dreams as wings, we chase the night.
Our spirits free, like birds in air,
In ecstasy, we shed our care.

The mountains call, the rivers hum,
To nature's beat, we dance and run.
Each moment lived, a cherished spree,
In joyful leaps, we find the key.

With laughter loud, we greet the dawn,
In every heart, we're never drawn.
Together bound, we lose all fear,
In ecstasy, we hold what's dear.

The world is vast, a playground wide,
With open hearts, we take the ride.
In every breath, our souls ignite,
As free spirits, we embrace the light.

A Canvas of Laughter

Each smile we share, a brushstroke bright,
On life's canvas, we spread delight.
With laughter loud, our colors blend,
In joyous hues, our troubles mend.

The little jokes, the memories made,
In playful moments, fears do fade.
With every giggle, joy takes flight,
A masterpiece that feels so right.

The canvas flows, with stories told,
In vibrant shades, our hearts unfold.
Through laughter's art, we weave our tale,
In every stroke, we shall not fail.

With friends beside, our hearts align,
In this creation, life's design.
With laughter's touch, we paint the way,
A canvas brightens every day.

Whirlwinds of Wonder

In the dance of leaves that soar,
Dreams awaken, spirits roar.
Every twirl, a story spun,
In the whirlwinds, hope begun.

Colors blend in skies so bright,
Whirling shadows, pure delight.
Nature's song, a sweet refrain,
In the chaos, we find gain.

Mysteries in the air we chase,
Winds of change, a warm embrace.
Through the storms, we learn to fly,
In the wonder, we touch the sky.

Hearts entwined, we share the ride,
In this tempest, love can't hide.
Whirlwinds swirl, and we belong,
In their arms, we feel how strong.

Flickers of Freedom

Candles whisper in the night,
Flickers dance, a brave delight.
In their glow, our dreams take flight,
Freedom sparkles, pure and bright.

Chains that bind begin to break,
As the dawn begins to wake.
Voices rise in sweet refrain,
Flickers free from every chain.

Through the shadows, we will roam,
Finding peace, our hearts at home.
Each small spark builds to a flame,
In this light, we share our name.

Together we will forge the way,
In these flickers, hope will stay.
Through the dark, we claim the fight,
In our hearts, we find the light.

In the Embrace of Laughter

Joyful echoes fill the air,
Laughter dances everywhere.
With each chuckle, hearts are free,
In this space, we simply be.

Soft and warm, it wraps around,
Comfort found in every sound.
In the embrace of shared delight,
Laughter glows, our souls ignite.

Moments glimmer, fleeting fast,
Memories built that ever last.
In each smile, a spark we find,
Binding us, our hearts aligned.

Together we create the song,
In this laughter, we belong.
With each giggle, troubles cease,
In our joy, we find our peace.

The Joyful Journey

Step by step, our paths unfold,
Stories waiting to be told.
Every moment, rich and sweet,
In the journey, life's heartbeat.

Mountains rise, and rivers flow,
Through the valleys, we shall go.
With open hearts and hopeful dreams,
Life's adventure, bursting seams.

In the laughter and the tears,
We will conquer all our fears.
Hand in hand, we'll face the dawn,
In this journey, we are drawn.

Every turn, a chance to grow,
In our souls, the light will glow.
Together we'll embrace our fate,
In this journey, love awaits.

The Heart's Bright Melody

In whispers soft, the heart does sing,
A tune of joy, a gentle spring.
Each beat a note, a sweet refrain,
It dances light, through joy and pain.

With every breath, the music flows,
A harmony that softly grows.
In shadows deep, its echo calls,
A vibrant sound that never falls.

Happiness wrapped in a tender grace,
Bright chords of love begin to trace.
Together as one, in perfect time,
Our hearts compose a love sublime.

So let us sing, no fear or dread,
For in our hearts, the light is spread.
A melody that always stays,
To guide us through our winding ways.

Embrace of the Positive

In every dawn, a chance to smile,
Embrace the light and walk awhile.
The world is bright, a canvas true,
Paint every dream in vibrant hue.

With open hearts, we share the grace,
Empowering love, we find our place.
A simple word, a kind embrace,
Can change a life, uplift the pace.

In every storm, we seek the sun,
Together strong, we overcome.
For every tear a lesson learned,
In positive light, our spirits turned.

So let us shine, through thick and thin,
With hands held tight, we create win.
In kindness shown, we'll always find,
The joy that keeps our hearts aligned.

Sunbeams Through the Window

A golden ray breaks through the glass,
Illuminates the world, so vast.
In morning light, the shadows flee,
Creating warmth, setting us free.

Each little glow, a story unfolds,
Of dreams and hopes, of ages old.
Dancing across the wooden floor,
Whispers of light, forevermore.

Through leaves and branches, light cascades,
In gentle waves, the darkness fades.
As sunbeams touch each hidden space,
They bring forth joy and sweet embrace.

Let every beam a promise be,
A sign of love, eternally.
In every dawn, new life begins,
With sunlit dreams and whispered winds.

The Glee of Little Things

A fleeting breeze that stirs the leaves,
A gentle sound that nature weaves.
A smile from one, a dance of fate,
In little joys we celebrate.

The laughter shared, a simple word,
A fleeting moment, life unheard.
A flower bloom, a starry night,
In tiny wonders, hearts take flight.

A cup of tea, a favorite song,
In little things, we all belong.
A tender glance, a warm embrace,
In life's small joys, we find our place.

So raise a glass to all that's small,
For in these moments, we find it all.
In every step, let joy take wing,
And cherish life in little things.

The Tapestry of Light

Threads of gold weave through the air,
Whispers of dawn, a gentle care.
Colors dance upon the dawn,
Painting dreams as night is gone.

Every shadow finds its place,
Kissed by warmth, a soft embrace.
Intertwined in fate's sweet thread,
In this glow, all fears are shed.

Stars adorn the evening sky,
Lighting paths as hours fly.
With each hue, a story spun,
A harmony as day is done.

In the silence, light will guide,
Through the dark, it will abide.
Tapestries woven, hearts ignite,
In the calm, we find our light.

Musings of Merriness

Laughter echoes in the air,
Joyful spirits everywhere.
Moments fleeting, yet so bright,
Chasing dreams with pure delight.

Bubbles float on a soft breeze,
Whispers mingle with the trees.
Every smile, a gift bestowed,
In mirth's embrace, our hearts explode.

Dancing shadows play on walls,
Fleeting time, yet merriness calls.
Gather 'round, let stories flow,
In this warmth, let love grow.

As the sun starts to set low,
We share tales of what we know.
With each laugh, our spirits soar,
Merriness blooms forevermore.

Cherishing the Now

In this moment, time stands still,
Hearts entwined, we feel the thrill.
Each breath taken, a gift so rare,
Cherish it with utmost care.

The world spins on, yet here we stay,
Lost in twilight's soft ballet.
Hand in hand, we dare to dream,
Each heartbeat flows like a stream.

Memories woven, tender threads,
In the now, our spirit spreads.
Let's pause here, let silence sing,
In this moment, love takes wing.

Embrace the present, hold it tight,
Let worries fade in gentle light.
For in this space, we truly know,
Life's beauty lies in cherishing now.

Luminous Paths

Beneath the stars, our stories blend,
On luminous paths, our spirits mend.
Every step, a dance of fate,
Drawing us to love's soft gate.

Moonlit trails twist and twine,
Guided by a spark divine.
With each glow, we find our way,
In this journey, night meets day.

Shadows fade as hopes arise,
Casting dreams across the skies.
Together we shall brave the night,
On these paths, we find our light.

With every heartbeat, courage grows,
Through the darkness, the heart knows.
Luminous paths that shine so bright,
Lead us home, a guiding light.

The Aroma of Fresh Beginnings

In dawn's embrace, a soft light glows,
The air is sweet with the bloom of rose.
New dreams arise, like morning dew,
Each breath a promise, fresh and true.

A path unfolds, where hope aligns,
With whispered winds, the heart defines.
A canvas blank, with colors bright,
In every moment, pure delight.

Seeds of courage take their place,
In gardens rich, through time and space.
The scent of change, it fills the air,
Awakening dreams, beyond compare.

So let us tread this vibrant way,
With open hearts, come what may.
The aroma of new paths we seek,
In every heartbeat, fresh and weak.

Harmony in the Heart

In gentle tones, our spirits blend,
Creating songs that never end.
With every glance, a silent vow,
To dance together, here and now.

The laughter shared, a melody,
That resonates in harmony.
In whispered dreams beneath the stars,
We find our peace, despite the scars.

When shadows fall and doubts arise,
We seek the light within our eyes.
For in this bond, we stand as one,
Two hearts, together, always run.

With every beat, we chart our way,
Through storms and calm, come what may.
In perfect sync, we start anew,
In harmony, just me and you.

Wings of Wonder

A feathered flight on whispers high,
With dreams that reach, like clouds in the sky.
In every flutter, stories unfold,
Of journeys vast, and treasures untold.

The world below fades into a blur,
As we embrace the flight of the spur.
In the rush of air, we feel the thrill,
With wings of wonder, we climb the hill.

The sunset paints a canvas bright,
With shades of gold, igniting the night.
In every turn, we find new views,
With every heartbeat, we chase our muse.

So let us soar on hopeful wings,
To discover all the joy life brings.
In wonder's grasp, we shall remain,
Through skies of blue, through joy and pain.

Gentle Waves of Contentment

The ocean sings a soothing song,
In rhythmic waves, where we belong.
Each tide that rolls, a sweet caress,
A calming touch, pure happiness.

Beneath the sun, we find our place,
With warm embrace, a soft embrace.
In sandy shores, our footprints stay,
As time flows gently, day by day.

The whispers of the sea remind,
To leave our worries far behind.
In every splash, in every sigh,
We feel the peace that drifts on by.

So let the waves wash over us,
In simple joys, we place our trust.
In gentle moments, hearts content,
We find our home, where love is sent.

Milton Keynes UK
Ingram Content Group UK Ltd.
UKHW051812101024
449294UK00007BA/70